THIS BOOK BELONGS TO:

○○○○○○○○○○○○○○○○○○○○○○○○○○○○○○

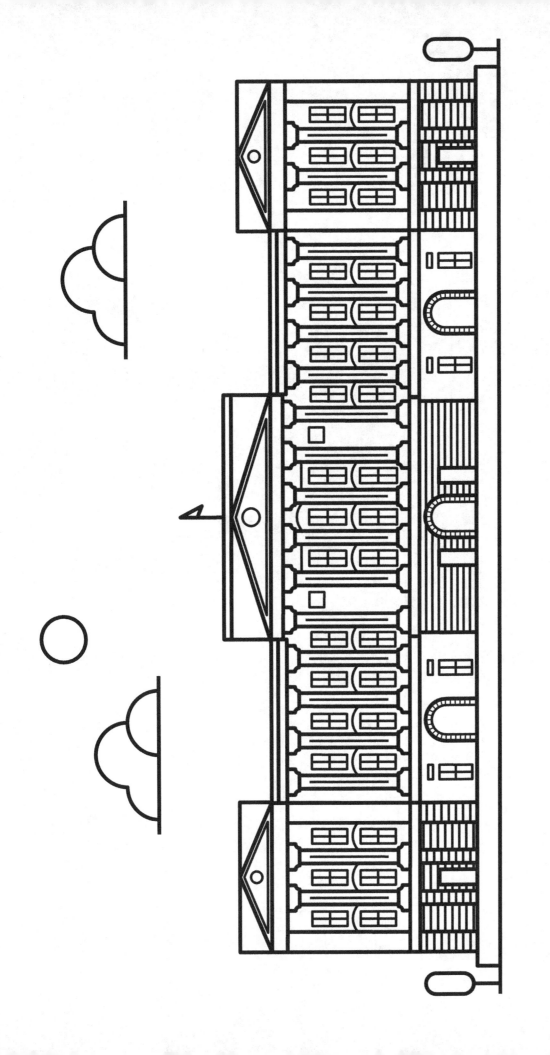

Buckingham Palace

Tower Bridge

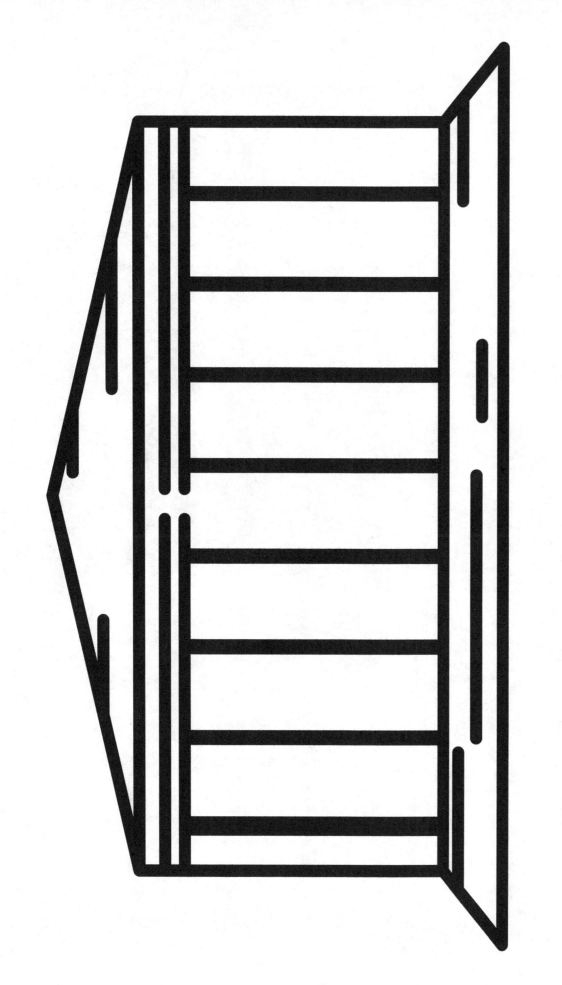

British Museum

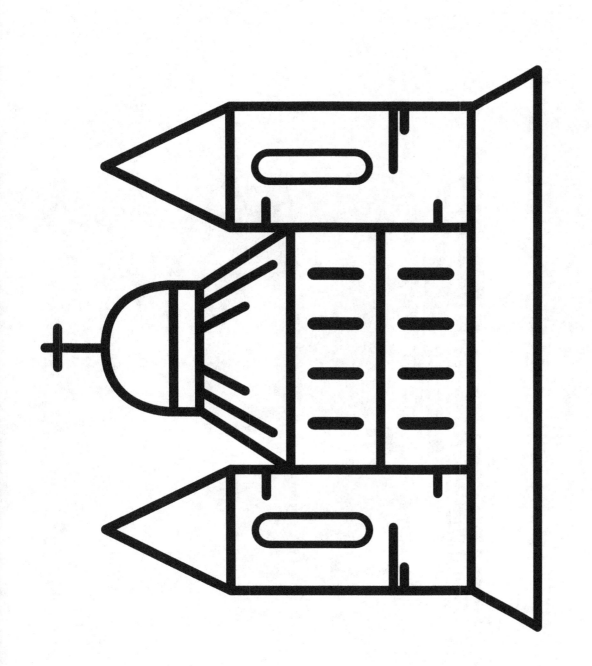

St. Paul's Cathedral

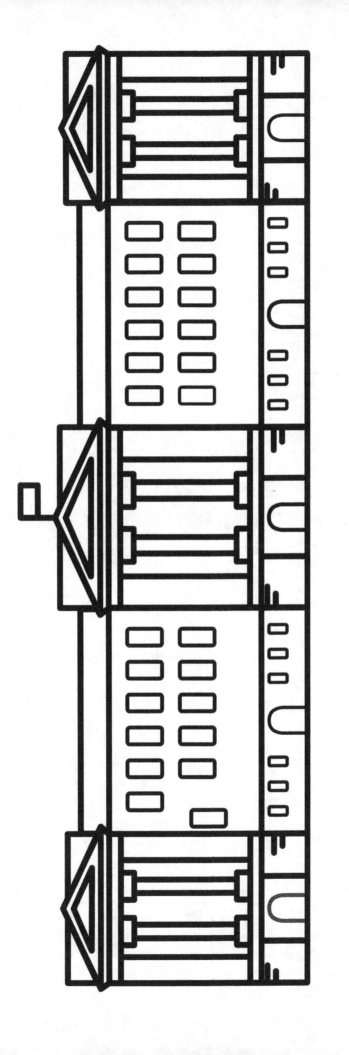

Westminter Palace

Westminster Abbey

LONDON EYE

BIG

BEN

BLACK CAB

QUEEN'S GUARD

RED TELEPHONE BOOTH

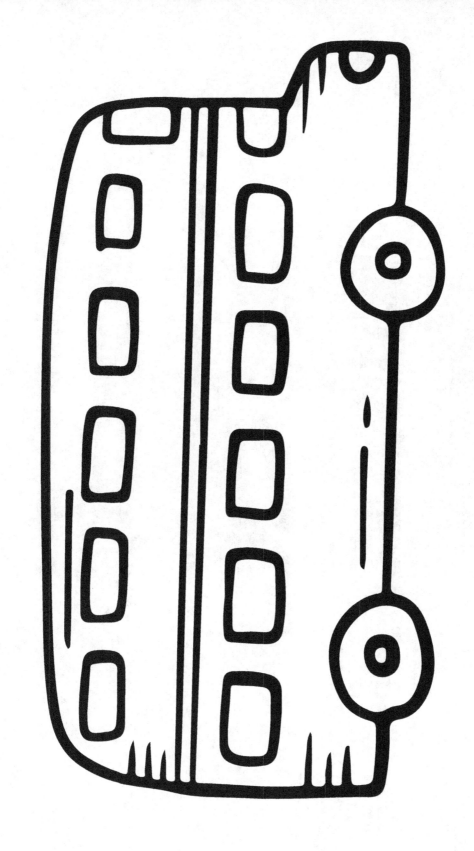

DOUBLE DECKER BUS

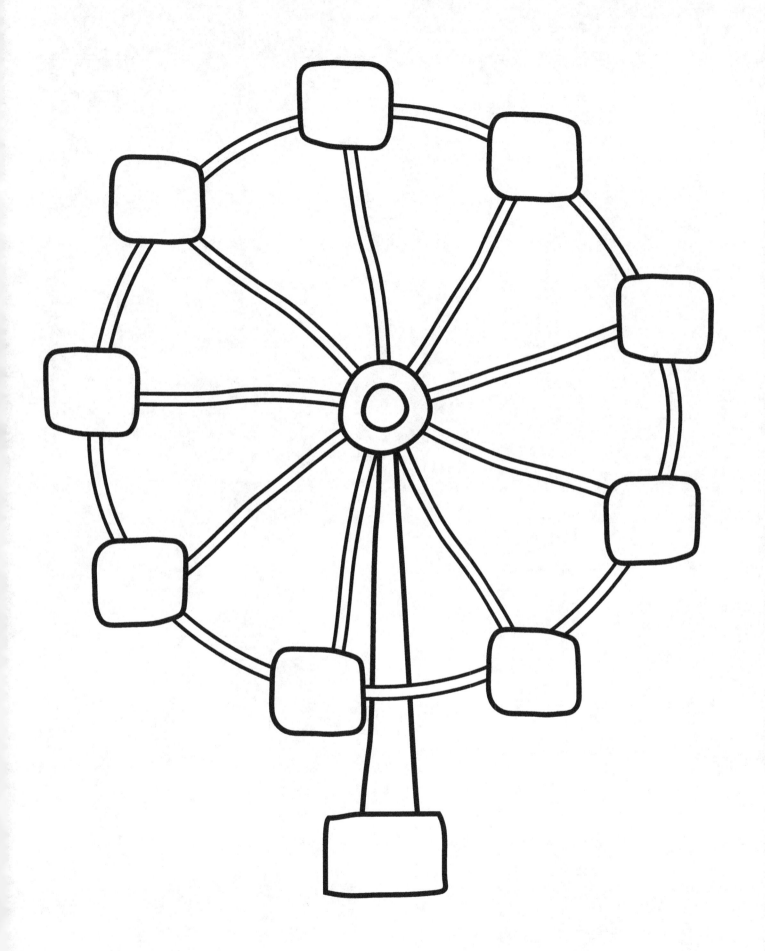

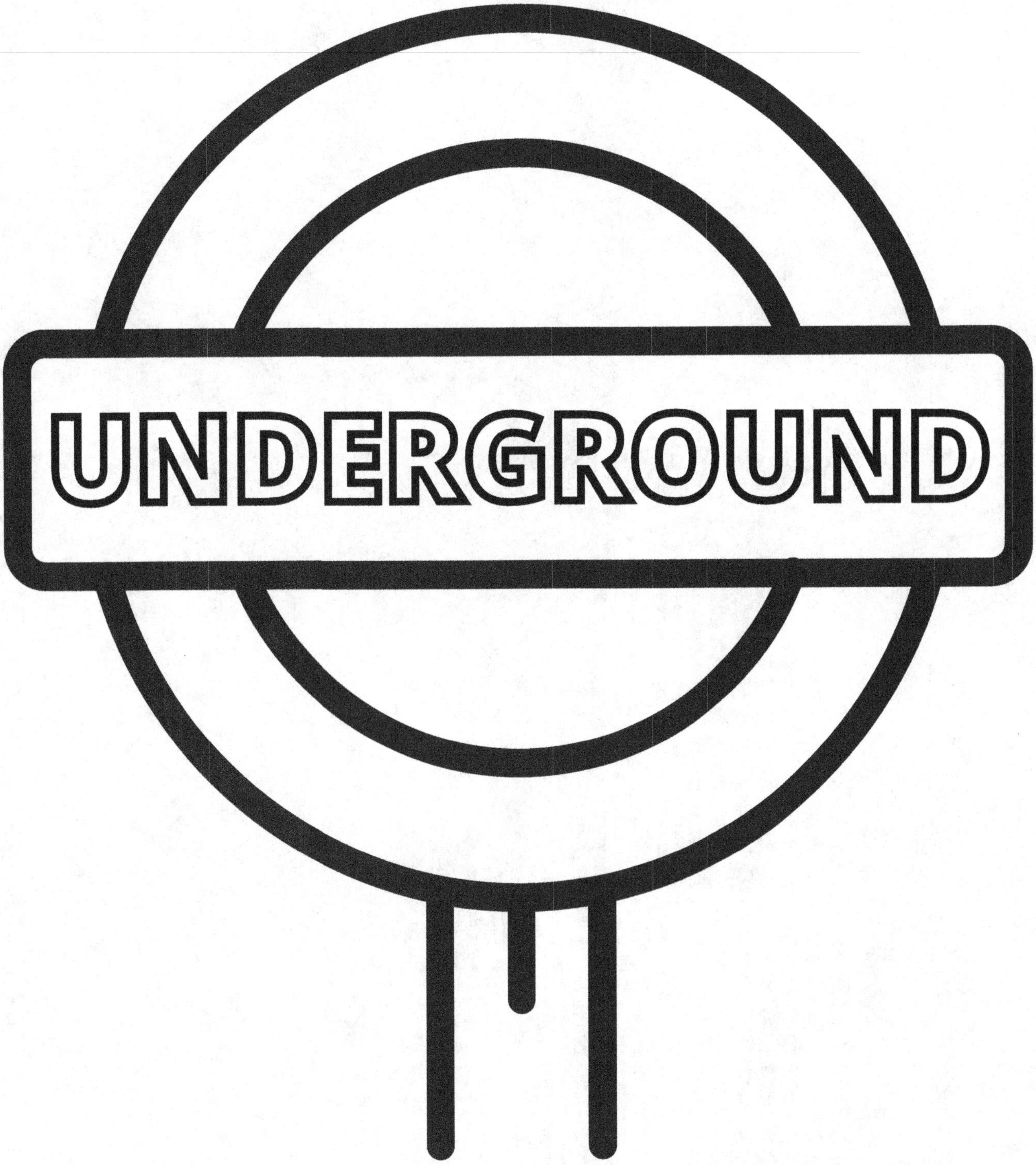
UNDERGROUND

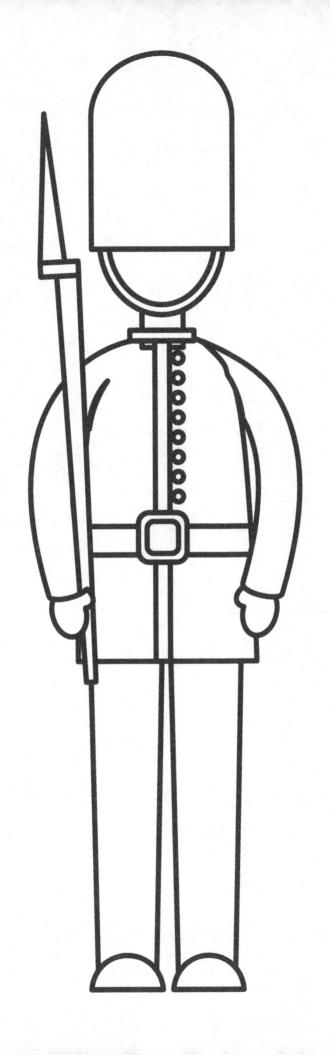

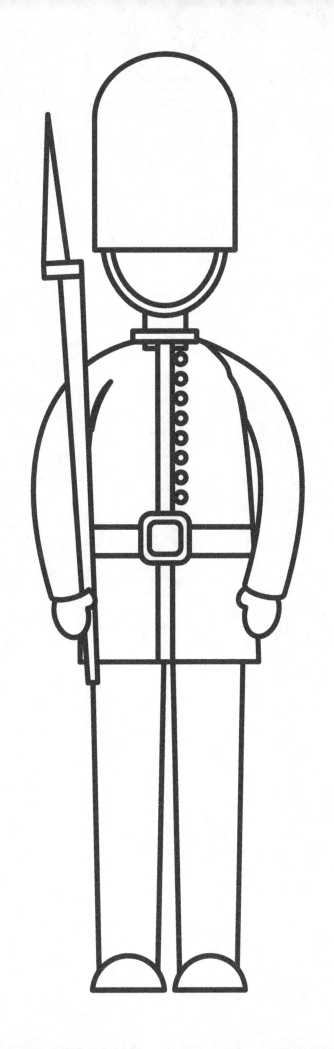

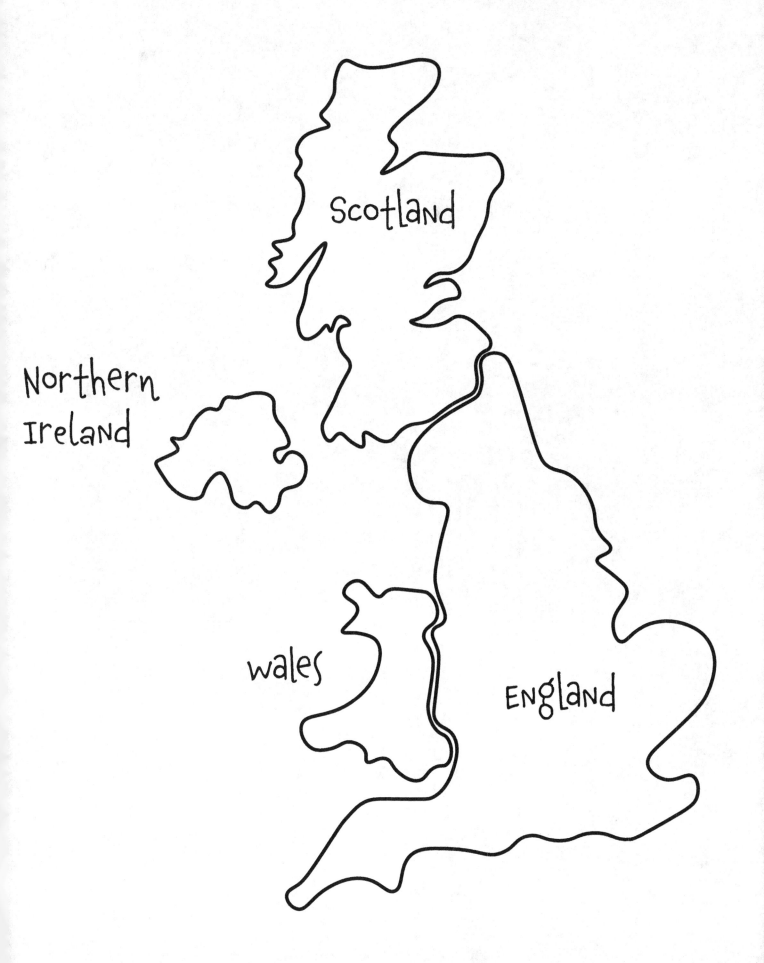

London

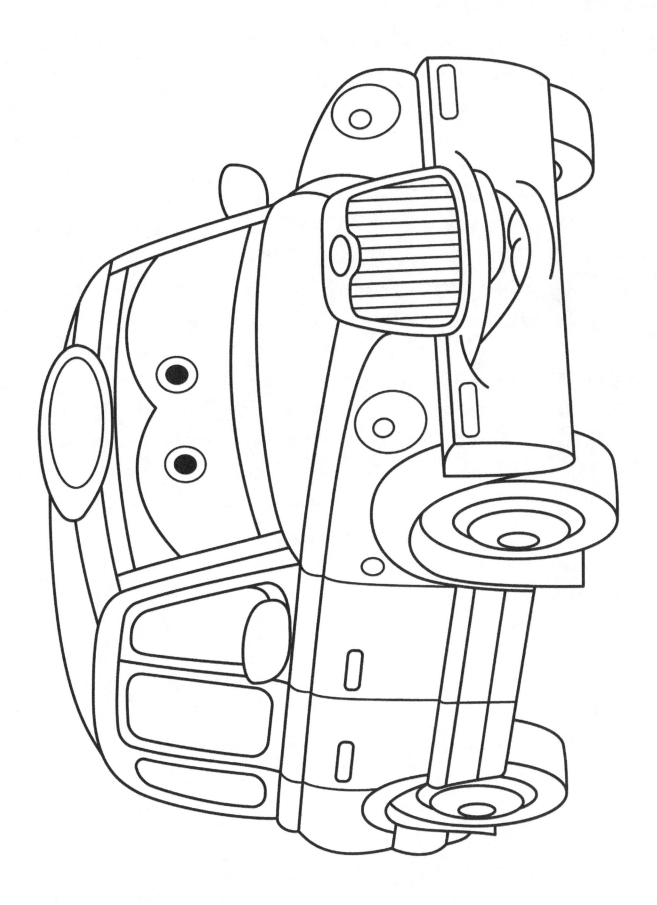

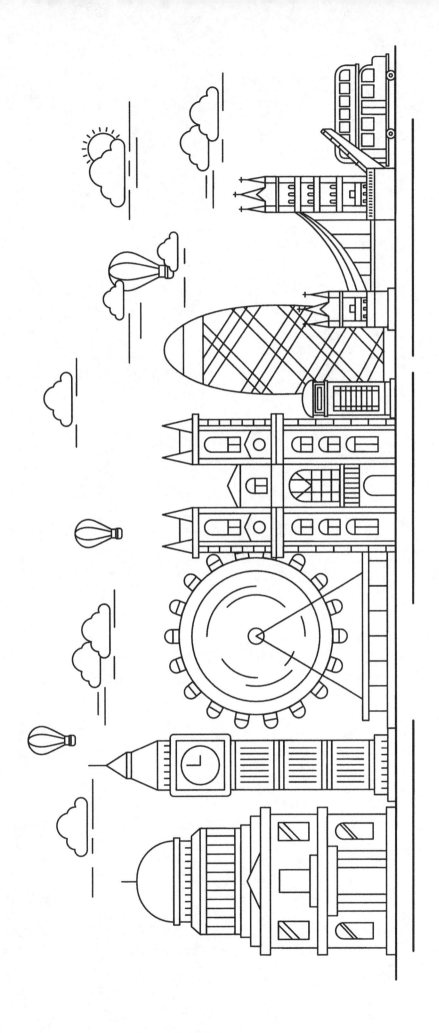

LONDON

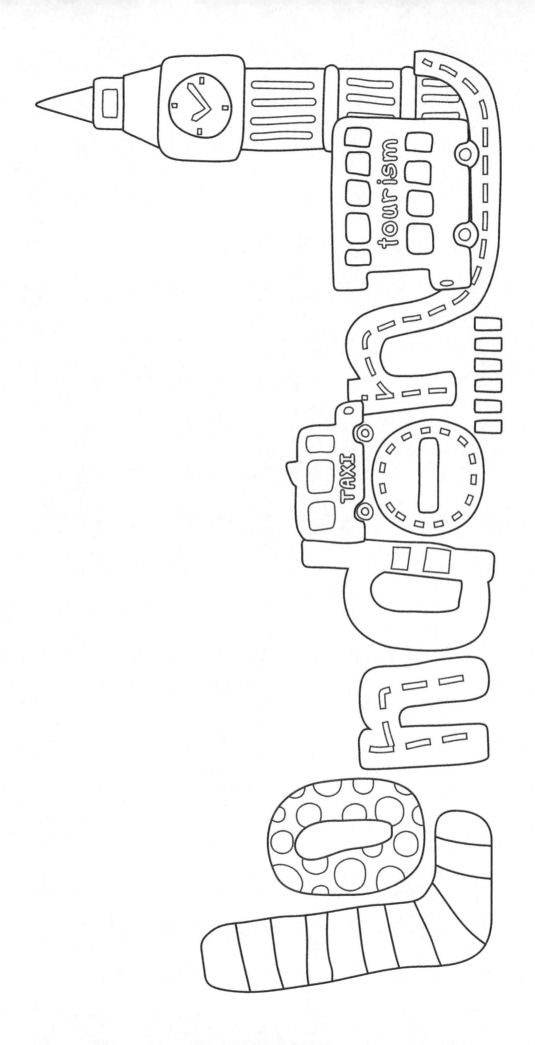

LONDON

Dear customer!

Thank you for your recent purchase.

We hope you love it!

If you do, would you consider posting an online review?
This helps us to continue providing great products and helps
potential buyers to make confident decisions.

Thank you in advance for your review and for being a
preferred customer.

See more of my books

Caroline Storgett

Made in the USA
Middletown, DE
17 October 2023

41003490R00051